JOURNEY 101
STEPS TO THE LIFE GOD INTENDS

SERVING GOD

Leader Guide

JOURNEY 101
STEPS TO THE LIFE GOD INTENDS

This three-part basic faith course is designed to teach what it means to know, love, and serve God. Each of the three separate, interactive six-week studies uses a group-teaching format, combining video teaching and small-group table breakouts. The three studies include:

KNOWING GOD. Explore the good news of the Bible and discover Bible study tools and resources to deepen your understanding of God and the Scriptures.

LOVING GOD. Experience spiritual transformation through spiritual practices that will help you fall more in love with God and grow in your relationship with God and others.

SERVING GOD. Understand the biblical context for service that will enable you to use your hands, your time, and your spiritual gifts to serve others and share Christ.

COMPONENTS

Participant Guide (one for each study)—Each includes interactive guides for six sessions with space for responding to questions and activities and recording personal reflections.

Leader Guide (one for each study)—Each includes complete session guides with leader helps for facilitating a six-week study.

Journey 101 Daily Readings—Serves as the devotional companion for the entire three-part Journey 101 series. Ninety devotions (thirty devotions per study).

DVD—Three-disc set (120 minutes per DVD/study; 360 minutes total).

Preview Book—Provides an overview of the topics covered in the entire three-part Journey 101 course.

Leader Kit—One each of the components listed above.

SERVING GOD

LEADER GUIDE

Carol Cartmill
Jeff Kirby
Michelle Kirby

Abingdon Press

Nashville

JOURNEY 101: SERVING GOD

Leader Guide

Copyright © 2013 by Abingdon Press

All rights reserved.

This book is printed on acid-free paper.

ISBN 9-781-4267-6584-1

13 14 15 16 17 18 19 20 21 22—10 9 8 7 6 5 4 3 2 1

MANUFACTURED IN THE UNITED STATES OF AMERICA

CONTENTS

Introduction

THE JOURNEY

When we give our lives to Jesus Christ and commit to follow him, we embark on a lifelong journey of knowing, loving, and serving God. Growing as a Christian and becoming a committed follower of Jesus Christ means:

knowing God by becoming theologically informed,

loving God and experiencing spiritual transformation, and

serving God by using our hands to serve others and share Christ.

Journey 101 is a three-part course designed to help you guide individuals on this journey of knowing, loving, and serving God. The destination or goal is to help participants engage in the discipleship journey and move toward becoming deeply committed Christians—people who know, love, and serve God with increasing passion and dedication. As you lead participants toward this destination, creating an atmosphere where they can experience growth and find support, you will help to provide answers to the following questions:

- How does a deeply committed Christian grow to know God more deeply?

- How would our lives be transformed if we loved God with the fullness of our hearts?

- How should we, as deeply committed Christians, be serving in the world?

To help you and your group know that you are on the right track to your destination, we have identified fifteen markers to guide you. We call these markers the fifteen core traits of a deeply committed Christian. These traits paint a picture of what it looks like to live as a deeply committed follower of

Jesus Christ. Each study in the Journey 101 series focuses on five of these core traits. (See pages 12-13 for detailed descriptions of these core traits.)

Because starting any journey can sometimes be daunting, particularly for those who may be new to the faith or the church (or your church in particular), Journey 101 serves as a navigation system that provides directions, routes, and traveling companions to support and encourage participants along the way. Here is a description of what your group will learn in each study:

KNOWING GOD

- Gain a better understanding of the essentials of the Christian faith.

- Experience new Bible study tools and resources.

- Discover more about the church.

- Discuss ethics and our Christian response to life's decisions.

- Understand more about God's will for your life.

LOVING GOD

- Learn about the Holy Spirit's transforming power in our lives.

- Understand more about what it means to love God with all your heart, soul, mind, and strength and to love your neighbor as you love yourself (Luke 10:27).

- Understand and experience key spiritual practices including Bible study, prayer, worship, fasting, guidance, and journaling.

- Learn to recognize the "fruit" of God's transforming activity in our lives—love, joy, peace, patience, kindness, generosity, gentleness, faithfulness, and self-control.

SERVING GOD

- Focus on the Bible's concern for the poor and for justice while learning how to be instruments of God's love in a broken, hurting world.

- Learn how to share the good news of Jesus in loving, winsome, and non-judgmental ways.

- Understand spiritual gifts and talents and how to use those gifts to bless others and build up the body of Christ.

- Learn how our money and material possessions are not a measure of success or a means of self-gratification, but a resource to responsibly use to glorify God.

- View time as a gift from God, to be used in keeping with God's purposes, avoiding compulsive busyness and submitting our calendars to God's guiding and control.

These separate, six-week studies combine to create a complete discipleship course. Although it is recommended that participants take each study, there is no set order in which they must be completed.

ABOUT THE PARTICIPANT GUIDE

Because Journey 101 is designed as an in-class experience (everything takes place in the group setting; there is no homework to be done outside of class), the participant guide is every participant's "map" for the weekly group experience. Communicate to participants the importance of bringing their participant guides to each class, along with a pen or pencil and a Bible. Be sure to have extra writing utensils and Bibles on hand for those who forget or who may not own a Bible.

Invite participants to follow along in their participant guides as you lead them through each session. Questions and activities that are to be answered or completed in the book are highlighted in bold type. Encourage group members to write in their participant guides as directed so that they will have their own personal record of their journey and the insights they gained along the way.

Though no homework is involved, participants may wish to use the devotional companion, *Journey 101 Daily Readings*, in their private devotions while completing the three-part Journey 101 series. These devotions will help to enrich their understanding and application of what they are learning in class.

ABOUT THIS LEADER GUIDE

This leader guide provides outlines for six group sessions, each structured for 90 minutes. If desired, you may adapt the format for a 60-minute or 120-minute session by making the adjustments outlined below:

Original 90-minute Format

Welcome—5 minutes
Connect—5 minutes
Reflect—3-5 minutes
Video Highlights—10 minutes

Group Discussion—10 minutes
Video Highlights—10 minutes
Group Discussion—10 minutes
Video Highlights—10 minutes
Group Discussion—10 minutes
Review—3-5 minutes
Closing—5 minutes
Pray Together—5 minutes

Adapted 60-Minute Format

Welcome and Connect (combined and abbreviated)—5 minutes
Reflect—3 minutes
Video Highlights—10 minutes
Group Discussion (abbreviated)—5 minutes
Video Highlights—10 minutes
Group Discussion (abbreviated)—5 minutes
Video Highlights—10 minutes
Group Discussion (abbreviated)—5 minutes
Review—2 minutes
Closing and Prayer (combined and abbreviated)—5 minutes

Adapted 120-Minute Format

Welcome—5 minutes
Connect—10 minutes
Reflect—3-5 minutes
Video Highlights - 10 minutes
Group Discussion - 15 minutes
Video Highlights - 10 minutes
Group Discussion - 15 minutes
Video Highlights - 10 minutes
Group Discussion - 15 minutes
Review—10 minutes
Closing—5 minutes
Pray Together—10 minutes

Whichever format you choose, each session plan follows the same order. After welcoming participants and offering a prayer, you will lead participants through a get-to-know-you activity followed by a brief personal reflection exercise. Next, you will play three video segments (8-10 minutes each), pausing after each for group discussion. This is the primary "teaching time" of the session. The videos present the content while the group discussion helps participants to process it and make application. Note that more questions are provided than you may have time to cover. Select additional questions that you want to cover as time allows. Encourage participants to reflect on the other questions on their own.

After the final group discussion, you will briefly review the main points of the session and ask a couple of key comprehension questions. As the session draws to a close, you will invite participants to respond to the lesson in a closing activity. Finally, end the session with a time of prayer.

We believe that nothing in the world will bring you greater joy, greater challenge, and greater meaning than the journey into life as God intended us to live it. As you begin the journey, open yourself to what God has to teach you through the Scriptures, prayer, and the guidance of the Holy Spirit.

FIFTEEN CORE TRAITS OF A DEEPLY COMMITTED CHRISTIAN

KNOWING GOD

Christian Essentials—Deeply committed Christians understand the essential gospel on which most Christians agree, across denominational lines and centuries, expressed in historic creeds such as the Apostles' and Nicene creeds, and can share the gospel intelligently with non-Christian friends.

Bible Understanding—Deeply committed Christians know the grand sweep of the Bible's story of salvation, including a basic time line of biblical events. They understand the divine/human nature of the Bible and know how to read it, not merely as an ancient document or a reference book of spiritual answers, but for personal spiritual growth.

Church/Denomination—Deeply committed Christians value the church as the body of Christ, God's people journeying in community, and know the teachings characteristic of their particular denomination.

Basic Christian Ethics—Deeply committed Christians understand how to apply their Christian faith to important ethical issues and are committed to living out Christian ethical principles such as justice, integrity, peace, and responsibility for the well-being of others.

Knowing God's Will—Deeply committed Christians know the broad scope of God's purpose for human beings, and have a growing sense of how to discern God's will for their lives through prayer, Bible study, and the wisdom of other Christians.

LOVING GOD

Surrender—Deeply committed Christians surrender the control of every aspect of their lives to Jesus, repent of sin, set aside their own desires and sense of importance, and offer their lives in obedient service to God.

Transformation—Deeply committed Christians are being continually transformed by the power of the Holy Spirit, and sense that power molding their values, priorities, and relationships into more Christlike patterns.

Spiritual Disciplines—Deeply committed Christians practice various spiritual disciplines (e.g., prayer, Bible reading, worship, solitude, meditation, fasting) as a means of surrendering to Jesus and opening their lives to the Holy Spirit's transforming activity.

Fruit of the Spirit—Deeply committed Christians are continually growing in the inner qualities and outward actions identified as "the fruit of the Spirit" in Galatians 5:22-23 (NRSV): "love, joy, peace, patience, kindness, generosity, faithfulness, gentleness, and self-control."

Authentic Community—Deeply committed Christians share their faith journeys with groups of Christian friends in mutual encouragement and accountability, developing spiritual honesty and trust through sharing and support.

SERVING GOD

Service to Others—Deeply committed Christians are instruments of God's love in a broken, hurting world, living lives of service to others with a strong (though not exclusive) focus on the Bible's concern for the poor and for justice.

Sharing Christ—Deeply committed Christians are eager to share the good news of Jesus in loving, winsome, and non-judgmental ways, and are ready to "give an answer to everyone who asks you to give the reason for the hope that you have" (1 Peter 3:15).

Spiritual Gifts/Talents—Deeply committed Christians understand clearly with "sober judgment" (Romans 12:3) which spiritual gifts and talents they have, and use those gifts to bless others and build up the body of Christ.

Financial Gifts—Deeply committed Christians view money and material possessions not as a measure of success or as a means of self-gratification, but as a resource for whose use they are responsible to God, and submit their financial lives to God's guiding and control.

Time—Deeply committed Christians see time as a gift from God to be used in keeping with God's purposes, avoid compulsive busyness, and submit their calendars to God's guiding and control.

HOW AND WHY WE SERVE GOD

BACKGROUND

Key Scripture

Jesus went through all the towns and villages, teaching in their synagogues, proclaiming the good news of the kingdom and healing every disease and sickness.

Matthew 9:35

Theme

Today you will explore with participants why and how we serve God as God's disciples. The material in this session will help participants discover that in order to find out what matters to God, we can look to Jesus. We serve God by doing the things that Jesus did: loving others by acting with justice, mercy, compassion, and care. In this session, participants will learn that every journey with God leads to other people.

Main Points

1. Every journey with God always leads to community.
2. Jesus teaches us how to serve.
3. We are called to serve the world as community—the church.

Core Trait

- Service to Others

WELCOME (5 MINUTES)

As participants gather, invite them to get some refreshments and find a seat. If you have more than six to eight participants, set up tables so that everyone may join a table group upon arriving. When it is time to begin, speak some words of welcome and lead an opening prayer. If you choose, you may want to use the following for opening words and prayer:

Welcome to our first session of Serving God. Today we will discover some whys and hows of serving others. I trust that God will meet us here and reveal new insights in our time together. Let us pray.

God, thank you for knowing us, for loving us, and for calling us to do your work in the world. Help us to see the world through your eyes and give us the courage to act when you call. In Jesus' name we pray. Amen.

After the prayer, introduce the learning objectives for the session (see the "Main Points" above).

CONNECT (5 MINUTES)

Now it's time for participants to connect. Refer participants to the "Connect" section in the participant guide and invite them to get to know one another better by sharing freely in response to the following questions and suggestions:

- Meet the people around your table. Share your name and how long you have attended this church.

- Find three things that everyone at your table has in common with one another.

- In what era—if other than your own—do you wish you had grown would you like to have grown up? Why?

- If it were possible for you to do something dangerous just once without risk, what would you do?

- If you had the means, how would you address the problem of homelessness?

REFLECT (3-5 MINUTES)

Point out the activity in the "Reflect" section of the participant guide.

Encourage participants to reflect on what they think it means to serve. Ask them to consider their willingness and availability at this moment in their lives. Invite them to mark the scale in their books and complete the sentence.

This activity is for personal reflection only and does not need to be shared or debriefed.

1 VIDEO: JOURNEYING WITH GOD LEADS TO OTHER PEOPLE (10 MINUTES)

Introduce the first DVD segment by explaining that, by nature, God is community and that we are called to be in community together to do God's work in the world. (Video highlights are included in the participant guide.)

1 GROUP DISCUSSION (10 MINUTES)

Discuss with your group the following questions and suggestions. Make sure that participants have Bibles readily available if they didn't bring them. Encourage participants to open their Bibles and have someone read aloud the Scriptures as you come to them.

1. Name some examples of how you experience community in your life (family, friends, church, the workplace, other).
2. Have someone read aloud part of Joseph's story found in Genesis 45:1-15. How did Joseph's journey lead to community?
3. What does it mean that we were created to be dependent on one another?
4. How do all journeys with God lead to community?

2 VIDEO: LEARN ABOUT SERVING FROM JESUS (10 MINUTES)

Introduce the second video segment by explaining that if we want to know what it means to serve, we can find the answer by looking at Jesus. (Video highlights are included in the participant guide.)

2 | GROUP DISCUSSION (10 MINUTES)

Discuss with your group the following questions.

1. What do you think it means that Jesus is "God with skin on"?
2. What do we know from Jesus' teaching and ministry about the importance of serving?
3. Have someone read aloud Luke 7:11-17. How does Jesus show compassion in this story? What does it tell us about his heart for hurting people?
4. When have you felt led to "suffer alongside" someone?
5. What would the world look like if all Christians lived out Jesus' example of serving?
6. How could you begin to serve like Jesus? To have compassion like Jesus? To love others like Jesus did?
7. Have someone read aloud Philippians 2:5-11. What is Jesus' attitude? How can we have the same attitude?

3 | VIDEO: THE CHURCH SERVES (10 MINUTES)

Introduce the final video segment by sharing that God calls the church to be the hands and feet of Jesus in the world—to do the good works that he called us to do. (Video highlights are included in the participant guide.)

3 | GROUP DISCUSSION (10 MINUTES)

Discuss with your group the following questions.

1. How have you seen the church at work in service to your community?
2. Why is it important to serve as part of a community?
3. How do you respond to the ideas shared in the video about doing good and helping the poor? What challenges you? What appeals to you? Why?
4. Have someone read aloud James 2:14-18. In your experience, how does faith lead to works? How has your faith led you to do good?
5. Have someone read aloud Galatians 5:22–6:2. In these verses, Paul suggests that it is grace that empowers the practice of doing good, which in

turn transforms the community. How has your Christian community been shaped by grace, and how has grace shaped your community's efforts to "do good" in the larger society?

6. What are some ways you have practiced the rule to "do good"? What challenges have you identified in your efforts to practice this rule?

Review (3-5 minutes)

Help to solidify the content with participants by inviting them to name the three main points covered in this session. Ask volunteers to name them in their own words, assisting them as necessary.

In this session, the main points were:

1. Every journey with God always leads to community.
2. Jesus teaches us how to serve.
3. We are called to serve the world as community—the church.

Ask the following questions:

1. How important do you think serving is to the life of a Christian? Why?
2. What ideas do you have for doing good works this week?

Closing (5 minutes)

Remind the participants that in the last video segment participants heard about how serving others changed Terri's life. Invite them to consider times when they served someone else. Ask them to share how those experiences changed them. Then have them begin to describe their own stories using the questions in the participant guide:

1. When did serving someone change you?
2. What happened as a result of your act of service?
3. How is your life a response to that change in you?

Pray Together (5 minutes)

Express gratitude for the commitment of the group members gathered to take this journey to serve God. Encourage them by promising to pray for them and be available to answer questions.

Ask participants to share joys and concerns for the week. After a few minutes, close your time with a prayer of your own, or invite group members to pray in unison the prayer that is printed in the participant guide:

Lord Jesus, we thank you for your amazing love. We ask that you would reveal to us the great needs around us and move our hearts to "doing." Show us how to love and care for one another in the same ways you did. May our love and knowledge of you, Lord, continue to grow and change the world. In Jesus' name. Amen.

WALKING IT OUT

Encourage participants to take what they have learned today and apply it in their daily lives by reflecting on the "Walking It Out" page in the participant guide throughout the coming week.

SERVING WITH TIME

BACKGROUND

Key Scripture

People can do nothing better than to eat and drink and find satisfaction in their toil. This too, I see, is from the hand of God.
Ecclesiastes 2:24 TNIV

Theme

Time is something that just about every one of us would say we need more of. Today, you'll invite participants to take a good look at how they spend their time, the ways in which time is a gift, and how we can use our time to love God and love others.

Main Points

1. God created time, and we are stewards of it.
2. God gave us a healthy rhythm of life.
3. We can love God and love others with our time.

Core Trait

- Time

Welcome (5 minutes)

As participants gather, invite them to get some refreshments and find a seat. If you have more than six to eight participants, set up tables so that everyone may join a table group upon arriving. When it is time to begin, speak some words of welcome and lead an opening prayer. If you choose, you may want to use the following for opening words and prayer:

> Welcome back to Serving God. Today we're going to take a good look at our time management. We'll hear that God actually created time as a gift for us. I know that God will meet us here to speak into our hearts and minds as we learn to give our time to God. Let us pray.

> Gracious God, we thank you for the gift of time and rest and joy. Thank you for all the blessings in our lives. Help us to discover ways to make more room in our lives for serving you. In Jesus' name we pray. Amen.

After the prayer, introduce the learning objectives for the session (see "Main Points" above).

Connect (5 minutes)

Now it's time for participants to connect. Refer participants to the "Connect" section in the participant guide and invite them to get to know one another better by sharing freely in response to the following questions:

- What is your favorite way to spend free time?
- If you had the ability to trade places with someone for a month, whom would you choose? Why?
- Which do you think is more essential to humanity, art or science? Why?
- Last week's lesson was on how and why we serve God. Have you experienced God speaking to you this week regarding ways you can serve?
- In your opinion, what do you think is the most significant problem facing our world?

Reflect (3-5 minutes)

Point out the activity in the "Reflect" section of the participant guide.

Explain that busyness is something we all struggle with. Everything feels important and we sometimes get confused about when to say yes and when to say no. Invite participants to make a list of their weekly engagements and commitments. Then they should circle the things that feel life-giving and put a box around things that bring a feeling of hurry or busyness. Have them consider whether they have any free time. Then ask them to dream about what they would do with free time if they found some.

This activity is for personal reflection only and does not need to be shared or debriefed.

1 VIDEO: STEWARDS OF TIME (10 MINUTES)

Introduce the first DVD segment by explaining that as God created day and night, God brought time into existence. Participants will discover that God created time and that they are called to be stewards of time, just as God called humans to steward the living things of the world. (Video highlights are included in the participant guide.)

1 GROUP DISCUSSION (10 MINUTES)

Discuss with your group the following questions. Make sure that participants have Bibles readily available if they didn't bring them. Encourage participants to open their Bibles and have someone read aloud the Scriptures as you come to them.

1. What do you think it means to be a good "steward" of your time?
2. Have you ever thought about stewarding your time in the same way that you steward your money or household? When is it easy to steward time? When is it difficult?
3. Have someone read aloud Luke 12:16-21. How does this parable speak to you about your priorities?
4. What does it look like to make the most of our "present reality in time"?

2 | VIDEO: A HEALTHY RHYTHM OF LIFE (10 MINUTES)

Introduce the second video segment by suggesting that God also created a rhythm of work and rest as a gift to us. We have a choice about how we manage our time and live out God's rhythm of life. (Video highlights are included in the participant guide.)

2 | GROUP DISCUSSION (10 MINUTES)

Discuss with your group the following questions.

1. Have someone read aloud Genesis 2:2-3. Why do you think God set the rhythm of time to include a day of rest?
2. Have someone read aloud Matthew 14:13-27. What do you think were some of Jesus' greatest challenges in creating some margin in his time?
3. Contrast Jesus' reactions to crises and demands with those of his disciples. How do they differ?
4. Describe the level of hurry in your life.
5. What would it take to ruthlessly eliminate hurry from your life?
6. Have someone read aloud all of Ecclesiastes 3. How does this passage challenge you to take hold of your time?

3 | VIDEO: LOVING GOD AND OTHERS WITH OUR TIME (10 MINUTES)

Introduce the final video segment by sharing that the use of our time is an act of loving God and serving others. Participants will be challenged to examine what they might need to clear out of their lives in order to eliminate hurry and create room for worship and service to God and others. (Video highlights are included in the participant guide.)

3 | GROUP DISCUSSION (10 MINUTES)

Discuss with your group the following questions.

1. What are the barriers you face when it comes to using your time in ways that bless others?
2. Which of the "prescriptions for restoring time margin" would be most helpful to you? Why?
3. How do you relate to time in your day-to-day life—in both healthy and unhealthy ways?
4. Reflect on a time when your heart wanted to help or serve in some way but you just couldn't find the time. How might you have been able to make time by cutting other things out of your schedule?
5. How is it true that God created time for our benefit? What are some of those benefits?
6. What adjustments can you make in your schedule in order to allow time for you to be "interrupted by God"?

REVIEW (3-5 MINUTES)

Help to solidify the content with participants by inviting them to name the three main points covered in this session. Ask volunteers to name them in their own words, assisting them as necessary.

In this session, the main points were:

1. God created time, and we are stewards of it.
2. God gave us a healthy rhythm of life.
3. We can love God and love others with our time.

Ask the following questions:

1. Why is it important that we learn to become stewards of our time instead of just letting life happen?
2. How can we serve God with our time?

CLOSING (5 MINUTES)

In the final DVD segment participants heard a story about Mary giving the gift of her time and making a difference in someone's life in a moment of need. Suggest that when we steward our time wisely, we are more available to make a difference in others' lives.

Ask participants to begin to consider how they might use their time to bless someone. Invite them to answer the questions in the participant guide:

1. In what ways could you give your time to bless another person?
2. Brainstorm some ideas for giving the gift of time and make notes about how you would organize your time to make it happen.

Pray Together (5 minutes)

Express gratitude for the commitment of the group members gathered to take this journey of serving God. Encourage them by promising to pray for them and be available to answer questions.

Ask participants to share joys and concerns for the week. After a few minutes, close your time with a prayer of your own, or invite group members to pray in unison the prayer that is printed in the participant guide:

God, thank you for the gift of time, and we thank you for showing us a rhythm for how we are to spend our time. We ask that your Holy Spirit will help us to use our time wisely, investing it in things that have meaning. Help us to be more available to you and to come into your presence to be refilled and refueled, just as Jesus modeled for us. Help us to take control of our calendars so that, when it really counts, we can be available to serve those that you place in our paths. In Jesus' name, we pray. Amen.

Walking It Out

Encourage participants to take what they have learned today and apply it in their daily lives by reflecting on the "Walking It Out" page in the participant guide throughout the coming week.

Session 3

GENEROSITY

BACKGROUND

Key Scripture

"For where your treasure is, there your heart will be also."
Matthew 6:21

Theme

Today you will explore generosity with participants. They will learn a process of resetting their financial journey and developing financial goals in order to become more generous. Point out that this session is not intended to get them to give more money to the church but to develop a lifestyle of generosity—the kind Jesus taught so much about.

Main Points

1. Jesus calls us to be generous with our money.
2. Financial freedom requires discipline and a plan.
3. We serve God by keeping our finances in order and giving freely.

Core Trait

- Financial Gifts

WELCOME (5 MINUTES)

As participants gather, invite them to get some refreshments and find a seat. If you have more than six to eight participants, set up tables so that everyone may join a table group upon arriving. When it is time to begin, speak some words of welcome and lead an opening prayer. If you choose, you may want to use the following for opening words and prayer:

Welcome back to Serving God. Today might be a little uncomfortable for some of you. Sometimes people can be a little leery of talking about money. But we're not just talking about giving to the church today. Today we are on a journey to discover what Jesus thinks about generosity and how we can live it out in our contexts and with our resources. I trust that God will meet us here. Let us pray.

Loving God, thank you for all of the generous blessings you have lavished upon us. You have been so very good to us. Help us to steward our finances and resources in such a way that we are free to give as you would call us to give. In Jesus' name we pray. Amen.

After the prayer, introduce the learning objectives for the session (see "Main Points" above).

CONNECT (5 MINUTES)

Now it's time for participants to connect. Refer participants to the "Connect" section in the participant guide and invite them to get to know one another better by sharing freely in response to the following questions and suggestions:

- Which would you prefer, to live near the beach or the mountains? Why?

- When choosing friends, what qualities do you think are most important?

- What adjustments have you made since last week regarding how you spend your time?

- If you had a million dollars to donate to a charity or cause of your choice, which charity or cause would you choose? Why?

REFLECT (3-5 MINUTES)

Point out the activity in the "Reflect" section of the participant guide. Invite participants to answer the questions there. Explain that when we receive generosity from others, we are often compelled to bless someone with our own acts of generosity.

This activity is for personal reflection only and does not need to be shared or debriefed.

1 VIDEO: JESUS ON GENEROSITY (10 MINUTES)

Introduce the first video segment by explaining that Jesus had a lot to say about generosity and money. (Video highlights are included in the participant guide.)

1 GROUP DISCUSSION (10 MINUTES)

Discuss with your group the following questions. Make sure that participants have Bibles readily available if they didn't bring them. Encourage participants to open their Bibles and have someone read aloud the Scriptures as you come to them.

1. Give one example of how someone's generosity changed or impacted your life.
2. Have someone read aloud Proverbs 22:9. What does the Scripture mean to you, and how does it apply to your life?
3. Have someone read aloud Matthew 6:21. What does this Scripture mean to you personally?
4. Assign one or more of the passages below to each person in your group. Then discuss the meaning of each Scripture and how it applies to our lives today.

   ○ Zacchaeus—Luke 19:7-9

   ○ Rich Young Ruler—Matthew 19:21-22

   ○ Poor Widow—Mark 12:41-44

   ○ Cheerful Giving—2 Corinthians 9:7

   ○ First Things—Matthew 6:33

   ○ Growth in Giving—2 Corinthians 8:12

○ Talents—Matthew 25:15

○ Blessed to Give—Acts 20:35

2 VIDEO: BIBLICAL PRINCIPLES FOR GIVING (10 MINUTES)

Introduce the second video segment by saying that now you will explore six biblical steps to resetting your financial journey. (Video highlights are included in the participant guide.)

2 GROUP DISCUSSION (10 MINUTES)

Discuss with your group the following questions.

1. Review each biblical principle from the video. For each principle, read aloud the principle, its corresponding Scripture, and its application. Discuss the ways each principle might lead to a generous life.
2. How easy or difficult are these principles to put into practice?
3. Do you currently budget or create spending plans? Why or why not?
4. Have you ever been in a situation where you wanted to give but didn't have the financial resources? What was that like?
5. How do these principles prepare us to be generous?

3 VIDEO: RESET YOUR FINANCIAL LIFE (10 MINUTES)

Introduce the final DVD segment by sharing that the church is called to be generous. In this video, participants will learn a tool for resetting their financial goals in order to give. This RESET worksheet can help the group rethink their finances and get themselves realigned financially. (Video highlights are included in the participant guide.)

RESET Worksheet[1]

What is God calling you to do? We all can improve in our spending, saving, and giving habits. Each of us can reset our personal, spiritual, and financial lives. Perhaps you will want to add other goals to the following.

1. Each day I will simply thank God for all my blessings. My goal for daily Bible reading and prayer will be _____ days each week.

2. I will seek contentment and live within my means each month. My goals will be to develop a monthly cash flow plan and to track my expenses so that I will spend _____ % of my income.

3. I will seek financial freedom from debt, especially credit card debt. My debt reduction goal for each month is $ _____.

4. I will seek to wisely manage the gifts God has given me, investing and saving for the future. My savings goal each month is $ _____.

5. I will worship God each week by giving _____% of my income, with tithing (and eventually giving beyond the tithe) being my goal.

---

3 GROUP DISCUSSION (10 MINUTES)

Discuss with your group the following questions:

1. How do you react when a pastor starts to talk about money? Why?
2. Based on what you heard in the video, why does a church need money?
3. Take a few minutes to complete the "RESET Worksheet" (above). How easy or difficult do you think it will be to fulfill each of the statements?
4. How do you think God might be calling you to change your spending habits so that you may give more?
5. Have someone read aloud 1 Timothy 6:18. What would it look like for you to be "rich in good deeds" and "generous and willing to share"?

Review (3-5 minutes)

Help to solidify the content with participants by inviting them to name the three main points covered in this session. Ask volunteers to name them in their own words, assisting them as necessary.

In this session, the main points were:

1. Jesus calls us to be generous with our money.
2. Financial freedom requires discipline and a plan.
3. We serve God by keeping our finances in order and giving freely.

Ask the following questions:

1. Why is financial freedom important for followers of Jesus?
2. How is God calling you to give?

Closing (5 minutes)

In the final video segment participants heard a story about David, who paid down a huge debt in order to be free to give. Ask them to begin to dream about how God might call them to give generously using the questions in the participant guide:

1. What is keeping you from being financially generous?
2. How can you take control of your finances in order to give more?
3. To whom or what would you give more if you had more to give?

Pray Together (5 minutes)

Express gratitude for the commitment of the group members gathered to take this journey of serving God. Encourage them by promising to pray for them and be available to answer questions.

Ask participants to share joys and concerns for the week. After a few minutes, close your time with a prayer of your own, or invite group members to pray in unison the prayer that is printed in the participant guide:

Heavenly Father, this can be a challenging topic for many of us. It brings up feelings of confusion, guilt, anger, pain, and even resentment. Help us to see all that we have as gifts from you, and help us to feel encouraged to give all that we can—not because we have to but because we are compelled by love to give. We ask this in your Son's name. Amen.

WALKING IT OUT

Encourage participants to take what they have learned today and apply it in their daily lives by reflecting on the "Walking It Out" page in the participant guide throughout the coming week.

SPIRITUAL GIFTS

Background

Key Scripture

> *Each of you should use whatever gift you have received to serve others, as faithful stewards of God's grace in its various forms.*
> 1 Peter 4:10

Theme

Today you will explore spiritual gifts with the participants. Perhaps they have never heard the language of spiritual gifts before, or they may be confused about what the gifts mean. In this session, you will help them understand the gifts and begin to identify what their spiritual gifts might be.

Main Points

1. The Holy Spirit is present in those who follow Christ.
2. Every believer has spiritual gifts.
3. Our spiritual gifts are meant to serve the church and, through the church, the world.

Core Traits

- Spiritual Gifs
- Talents

WELCOME (5 MINUTES)

As participants gather, invite them to get some refreshments and find a seat. If you have more than six to eight participants, set up tables so that everyone may join a table group upon arriving. When it is time to begin, speak some words of welcome and lead an opening prayer. If you choose, you may want to use the following for opening words and prayer:

As we turn our attention to spiritual gifts today, let's invite the Holy Spirit to come and remind us of our gifts, to name for us what God made us to do and be. Let us pray.

Holy God, we thank you that you place gifts within us to serve your church and the world. Help us to discover those gifts, to hone the gifts, and to learn where and when to practice them. In Jesus' name we pray. Amen.

After the prayer, introduce the learning objectives for the session (see "Main Points" above).

CONNECT (5 MINUTES)

Now it's time for participants to connect. Refer participants to the "Connect" section in the participant guide and invite them to get to know one another better by sharing freely in response to the following questions:

- What is the most beautiful place you have ever seen?
- If you had to leave this country, where would you choose to live?
- In what ways has last week's lesson on generosity impacted your life?
- When you were a child, what did you want to be when you grew up?
- What is one thing that people often say you are good at doing?

REFLECT (3-5 MINUTES)

Point out the activity in the "Reflect" section of the participant guide. Explain that God has given each of us one or more gifts. When we choose to follow Jesus, the Spirit places these gifts within us, which are meant to serve the church and the world. Invite participants to complete the statements in their participant guides and begin to discern their spiritual gifts.

I am naturally good at . . .

I have learned to be good at . . .

I experience great joy when I . . .

This activity is for personal reflection only and does not need to be shared or debriefed.

1 | VIDEO: THE BIRTH OF THE CHURCH (10 MINUTES)

Introduce the first video segment by sharing that when Jesus knew he would be going away from the disciples, he promised to send a Companion who would guide them. That Companion came in full force on the Day of Pentecost and brought about the birth of the church. We are a part of that community of Jesus' followers. (Video highlights are included in the participant guide.)

1 | GROUP DISCUSSION (10 MINUTES)

Discuss with your group the following questions. Make sure that participants have Bibles readily available if they didn't bring them. Encourage participants to open their Bibles and have someone read aloud the Scriptures as you come to them.

1. Have someone read aloud 1 Corinthians 12:7, 12-27. What role do spiritual gifts play in the life of an individual who is seeking to serve God?
2. Refer to the Scriptures from John and Acts in the video highlights and discuss the time line from Jesus' promise to send a Companion to the

time of the Holy Spirit's arrival at Pentecost. Follow the story and look for insights about what it meant for the disciples to follow Jesus when they knew he was going away.

3. Describe the scene you imagine when you read the story of Pentecost. What does that look like in your mind?
4. If the church is the chosen vehicle to bring hope to the world, how do we go about doing that?

2 VIDEO: FOUNDATIONAL BIBLE PASSAGES ON SPIRITUAL GIFTS (10 MINUTES)

Introduce the second video segment by explaining that participants have an assignment for this section. The video will introduce the assignment and then ask you to pause the DVD while groups fill in the chart printed in the participant guide and on page 39 of your leader guide. (Video highlights are included in the participant guide.)

2 GROUP DISCUSSION (10 MINUTES)

Discuss with your group the following questions and suggestions.

1. Refer to the Scriptures from the video highlights and discuss any questions or thoughts that came to mind when completing the preceding chart.
2. Describe the difference between talents and spiritual gifts.
3. How is the example of the body related to the functioning of spiritual gifts within the church?

3 VIDEO: DEVELOPING AND DISCOVERING SPIRITUAL GIFTS (10 MINUTES)

Introduce the final video segment by sharing that every Christian has one or more spiritual gifts. Have information available about any spiritual gifts classes offered at your church. Explain that although there isn't time for a full exploration of each gift now, participants are encouraged to take a class to fully discover their gifts. (Video highlights are included in the participant guide.)

3 | GROUP DISCUSSION (10 MINUTES)

Discuss with your group the following questions and suggestions.

1. In what ways does the church, and the community beyond its walls, benefit when its members discover, develop, and deploy their spiritual gifts?

2. Have someone read aloud 2 Timothy 1:6-7. What ongoing responsibility do we have with regard to our spiritual gifts? How might we go about doing what Paul advises?

3. Fear of failure is one obstacle that can keep us from using our gifts. Madeleine L'Engle wrote, "If I'm not free to fail, I'm not free to take risks, and everything in life that's worth doing involves a risk of failure. . . . I have to try, but I do not have to succeed. Following Christ has nothing to do with success as the world sees success."[1] If fear of failure is an obstacle for you, discuss how this quote makes you feel. If fear is not an obstacle, what threatens to keep you from serving God with your gifts?

REVIEW (3-5 MINUTES)

Help to solidify the content with participants by inviting them to name the three main points covered in this session. Ask volunteers to name them in their own words, assisting them as necessary.

In this session, the main points were:

1. The Holy Spirit is present in those who follow Christ.

2. Every believer has spiritual gifts.

3. Our spiritual gifts are meant to serve the church and, through the church, the world.

Ask the following questions:

1. Who gets spiritual gifts?

2. What is the purpose of spiritual gifts?

Passage	Who receives the gift?	For what purpose is the gift given?	What gifts are particularly named?
1 Corinthians 12			
Romans 12			
Ephesians 4			
1 Peter 4			

Closing (5 minutes)

Remind participants that in the last video segment they heard about John, who discovered his spiritual gifts and a greater passion for ministry in the church. Then remind them that we all have spiritual gifts with which to serve.

Ask participants to consider their own gifts by completing the following sections in the chart in the participant guide:

1. My Natural Abilities and Talents
2. What Brings Me Joy
3. What Stirs a Passion in Me

Pray Together (5 minutes)

Express gratitude for the commitment of the group members gathered to take this journey of serving God more fully. Encourage them by promising to pray for them and be available to answer questions.

Ask participants to share joys and concerns for the week. After a few minutes, close your time with a prayer of your own, or invite group members to pray in unison the prayer that is printed in the participant guide:

O God, sometimes we are amazed by the fact that you've left your work in the hands of ordinary people like us. And yet, just as Jesus said, you don't leave us as orphans or abandon us but give us the Holy Spirit, who works in us and through us to meet the needs of those around us. God, open our minds and our hearts and our very lives to the truth that we are all gifted people. Help us to discover our gifts and to deploy them to you and for you in service to others. In Christ's name we pray. Amen.

Walking It Out

Encourage participants to take what they have learned today and apply it in their daily lives by reflecting on the "Walking It Out" page in the participant guide throughout the coming week.

EVANGELISM

BACKGROUND

Key Scripture

Then Jesus came to them and said, "All authority in heaven and on earth has been given to me. Therefore go and make disciples of all nations, baptizing them in the name of the Father and of the Son and of the Holy Spirit, and teaching them to obey everything I have commanded you. And surely I am with you always, to the very end of the age."

Matthew 28:18-20

Theme

Today participants will explore a topic that can be intimidating: evangelism. Jesus has commanded and empowered the church to communicate his message to the world. Inspire participants to take on the challenge of taking the message of Jesus to the world.

Main Points

1. Christian conversion is a process.
2. The Holy Spirit creates hunger for God and highlights felt needs.
3. The Holy Spirit assists our repentance and faith.
4. The Holy Spirit moves through our network of family and friends.
5. The Holy Spirit reveals strategies.
6. The fruit of evangelism can be measured.
7. The Holy Spirit empowers our witness.

Core Trait

- Sharing Christ

WELCOME (5 MINUTES)

As participants gather, invite them to get some refreshments and find a seat. If you have more than six to eight participants, set up tables so that everyone may join a table group upon arriving. When it is time to begin, speak some words of welcome and lead an opening prayer. If you choose, you may want to use the following for opening words and prayer:

Welcome back to Serving God. Today we will explore evangelism and discover how we might take the gospel to the world. I know that God will show up here as we gather in his name. Let us pray.

Lord, thank you for your great sacrifice on our behalf. Thank you for believing in us so much that you would leave us with your work in the world. Thank you for the gift of the Spirit who inspires and equips us to take your gospel to the world. In Jesus' name we pray. Amen.

After the prayer, introduce the learning objectives for the session (see "Main Points" above).

CONNECT (5 MINUTES)

Now it's time for participants to connect. Refer participants to the "Connect" section in the participant guide and invite them to get to know one another better by sharing freely in response to the following questions:

- If you were offered front-row seats to any concert, who would you like to see?

- What is your favorite part of Thanksgiving dinner?

- Which do you think is more important, justice or forgiveness?

- Have you ever witnessed someone evangelizing in a manner that made you feel uncomfortable? How was this person going about sharing the message? Door-to-door? Shouting on a street corner? On television? Other? What about it was off-putting to you?

REFLECT (3-5 MINUTES)

Point out the activity in the "Reflect" section of the participant guide. Encourage participants to consider their faith stories. Ask them to write as if they were sharing the gospel with someone who had never heard it before. Challenge them to think of personal stories or examples about what following Jesus means.

This activity is for personal reflection only and does not need to be shared or debriefed.

1 VIDEO: EVANGELISM PRINCIPLES 1-2 (10 MINUTES)

Introduce the first video segment by explaining that today's video will cover seven important principles to remember about evangelism. To begin, you'll discover that conversion is a process. Refer the group members to to the "Engle Scale of Evangelism" in their particpant guides. (Video highlights are included in the participant guide.)

1 GROUP DISCUSSION (10 MINUTES)

Discuss with your group the following questions. Make sure that participants have Bibles readily available if they didn't bring them. Encourage participants to open their Bibles and have someone read aloud the Scriptures as you come to them. These questions are worded in a way that assumes the participants are already Christians. Be aware of this and be sensitive to anyone in your group who is still uncertain about his or her faith.

Share with your group:

1. What was your life like before you made the decision to follow Christ?

2. How did you come to know Christ?

3. How has knowing Christ made a difference in your life?

4. As you reflect on coming to faith in Christ, how do you see your conversion as a process?

5. How do you relate to the statistic that it takes twelve to fifteen significant encounters with the gospel for someone to come to faith? What were some of the significant encounters you experienced in your journey toward conversion?

6. Describe a time when you experienced the hunger or need in your heart brought about by the Holy Spirit. Did you struggle for significance? Have questions about the afterlife? Search for purpose?

7. Did you experience a "God-shaped vacuum" in your heart prior to meeting Jesus? If so, with what did you try to fill it?

2 VIDEO: EVANGELISM PRINCIPLES 3-5 (10 MINUTES)

Introduce the second video segment by sharing that the Holy Spirit helps us come to know Christ and to share the message of the gospel with others. (Video highlights are included in the participant guide.)

2 GROUP DISCUSSION (10 MINUTES)

Discuss with your group the following questions. When discussing questions 3 and 4, remind participants that it's OK if they do not have dramatic stories to share. Help them to reflect on how people, in both big and small ways, showed them the love of Christ and how they have showed Christ's love to others.

1. Have someone read aloud 2 Corinthians 5:16-21. How does Paul summarize the message of the Christian faith? How does knowing and understanding this information help you to articulate your own message to others?

2. Have someone read aloud Acts 1:8. How can we learn to grow in our ability and confidence to share our faith with others?

3. In what ways did the Holy Spirit use your family members or other relationships to reach you?

4. Has the Holy Spirit used you to reach someone in your family or network? If so, how?

5. Have you ever felt led by the Holy Spirit to share the gospel? If so, what strategy or idea did the Holy Spirit lead you to carry out?

3 | VIDEO: EVANGELISM PRINCIPLES 6-7 (10 MINUTES)

Introduce the final video segment by saying that God's desire is for churches to grow and thrive in number. (Video highlights are included in the participant guide.)

3 | GROUP DISCUSSION (10 MINUTES)

Discuss with your group the following questions and suggestions. (Special note: you may want to model for the group how to share their faith message by briefly sharing your own faith story. It is also important to know what to do when someone is ready to make a faith decision. Share a prayer that group members can use when they find themselves in that situation. It should be a simple prayer leading someone to entrust his or her life to Christ and expressing a desire to follow him.)

1. Identify a person in your life that you would like to see have a close, personal relationship with Christ. Drawing upon today's teaching, name one or more actions you can take in the coming week that will move you closer to sharing your faith with this person.
2. Do you agree that the fruit of evangelism matters, that it is quantifiable? Do numbers really matter? Why?
3. Take turns reading aloud Acts 1–2. Point out where evangelism is happening in the story. List any numbers noted about people coming to believe. What do we learn about evangelism in this story?
4. Brainstorm some strategies for sharing your faith. What places do you frequently visit? Who crosses your path regularly? How can you be prepared to share your faith when the Holy Spirit nudges you?
5. How will you serve God through the adventure of evangelism?

REVIEW (3-5 MINUTES)

Help to solidify the content with participants by inviting them to name the seven principles covered in this session. Ask volunteers to name them in their own words, assisting them as necessary.

In this session, the main points were:

1. Christian conversion is a process.
2. The Holy Spirit creates hunger for God and highlights felt needs.
3. The Holy Spirit assists our repentance and faith.
4. The Holy Spirit moves through our network of family and friends.
5. The Holy Spirit reveals strategies.
6. The fruit of evangelism can be measured.
7. The Holy Spirit empowers our witness.

CLOSING (5 MINUTES)

Remind participants that in the final video segment they heard how Jeff was instrumental in helping the man from Africa come to faith in Christ on an airplane. Invite them to make a list of people for whom they thank God—those who led them to Jesus. Then ask them to make a list of people for whom they might be that monumental influence.

PRAY TOGETHER (5 MINUTES)

Express gratitude for the commitment of the group members gathered to take this journey of serving God more fully. Encourage them by promising to pray for them and be available to answer questions.

Ask participants to share joys and concerns for the week. After a few minutes, close your time with a prayer of your own, or invite group members to pray in unison the prayer that is printed in the participant guide:

O God, we pray that these words might fall like seeds on receptive soil. Inspire us, transform our thinking, and fill us with new strategies so that others might come to know you. We thank you for the presence and power of the Holy Spirit, and for enabling us to be your witnesses. Lord, what a joy, what a thrill, what a responsibility you have given to us. Fill us afresh with your love and power. May the love of Christ compel us. For it's in his name we pray. Amen.

WALKING IT OUT

Encourage participants to take what they have learned today and apply it in their daily lives by reflecting on the "Walking It Out" page in the participant guide throughout the coming week.

SERVING GOD THROUGH SOCIAL SERVICE

BACKGROUND

Key Scripture

"Peace be with you! As the Father has sent me, so I am sending you."
John 20:21 CEB

Theme

Today you will explore with participants the call to serve God through social service and social action. Group members will be invited to dream of ways that they can jump into existing ministries or begin new ways of serving others in your community.

Main Points

1. Jesus calls his followers to be salt and light.
2. Choosing to serve God is one of the most meaningful choices you can ever make.
3. We can change the world with one act of love at a time.

Core Trait

- Service to Others

Welcome (5 minutes)

As participants gather, invite them to get some refreshments and find a seat. If you have more than six to eight participants, set up tables so that everyone may join a table group upon arriving. When it is time to begin, speak some words of welcome and lead an opening prayer. If you choose, you may want to use the following for opening words and prayer:

Welcome to our final session of Journey 101: Serving God. What a wonderful journey of discovery, community, and discipleship we have been on. I am certain that the seeds planted here will take root and grow in and through us and that God will use us to serve in many, many ways. Let us pray.

Loving God, we thank you that you are the ultimate example of serving. As we seek a servant's heart, point us to places where you would have us serve. Give us bravery to get out of our comfort zones. Give us courage to do tasks we thought we could never do. Give us eyes to see the world the way you do. In Jesus' name we pray. Amen.

After the prayer, introduce the learning objectives for the session (see the "Main Points" above).

Connect (5 minutes)

Now it's time for participants to connect. Refer participants to the "Connect" section in the participant guide and invite them to get to know one another better by sharing freely in response to the following questions and suggestions:

- Share your craziest "trying to get to church" story.

- If you could vacation anywhere in the world, where would you choose? Why?

- If it were possible and you had the means to do something wildly generous—anything—what would you choose to do?

- What do you see as needs in your community?

Reflect (3-5 minutes)

Point out the activity in the "Reflect" section of the participant guide. Remind participants that they completed a similar assessment in the first session. Encourage them to look back and see how they scored themselves. Suggest that, as their understanding of serving God has deepened, they might find themselves more willing to serve or to make time in their schedules. Ask participants to take a minute to complete the exercise individually, writing about what serving God means for them.

This activity is for personal reflection only and does not need to be shared or debriefed.

Video: The Call to Be Salt and Light (10 minutes)

Introduce the DVD segment by explaining that one of Jesus' most well-known teachings comes from the Sermon on the Mount, found in the Book of Matthew. In this sermon, Jesus teaches about what his kingdom really looks like and how his followers live in it. (Video highlights are included in the participant guide.)

Group Discussion (10 minutes)

Discuss with your group the following questions and suggestions. Make sure that participants have Bibles readily available if they didn't bring them. Encourage participants to open their Bibles and have someone read aloud the Scriptures as you come to them.

1. Reflect on this statement: "What Jesus was he still is, and what Jesus did he still does. But now he does it through you." What do you think of this idea? How does Jesus do what he did, even today, through you?

2. Have someone read aloud Matthew 5:13-16. What does it mean to be the "salt of the earth"?

3. What does it mean to be the "light of the world"?

4. The video offers John Wesley and William Wilberforce as examples of men who let their light shine. Can you name some other persons who were committed to the work of Jesus, even when it became difficult?

5. Who are the local heroes in your area who shine the light of Christ in their lives? What is unique about the way they live out their faith?

2 VIDEO: CHOOSING TO SERVE (10 MINUTES)

Introduce the DVD segment by explaining that following Jesus means taking some risks and stepping out of our comfort zones at times. Jesus calls us to serve and to act. Participants will learn the difference between social service and social action. (Video highlights are included in the participant guide.)

2 GROUP DISCUSSION (10 MINUTES)

Discuss with your group the following questions and suggestions.

1. Discuss the "withdraw and retreat" mentality. What makes us want to form a spiritual safe house?

2. Discuss the "engage in social service" church. What are some examples of churches that are known for their engagement in Christian service?

3. Discuss the difference between social service and social action. Name some examples of each.

4. Do you think one is better than the other? Why or why not?

5. When you consider serving in some way, what kind of service immediately comes to mind?

6. Would you say your heart leans more toward social service or social action? Why do you think this is so?

7. Tell a story about a time you were moved by serving others or by someone serving you.

3 VIDEO: CHANGING THE WORLD ONE ACT OF LOVE AT A TIME (10 MINUTES)

Introduce the final DVD segment by sharing that it's time for the groups to consider how they will jump in to serving God. Encourage participants to pay close attention to the stirring of the Holy Spirit as they hear about specific ministry ideas and dream about what they might be called to do. (Video highlights are included in the participant guide).

3 GROUP DISCUSSION (10 MINUTES)

Discuss with your group the following questions and suggestions. Remind participants that imitation is the highest form of flattery. With every question and every reflection, encourage them to consider how they might imitate Christ in their daily lives.

1. Have someone read aloud Hebrews 13:3. Discuss the implications this verse would have on your life if you lived it out.
2. In what ways does the church lose its credibility when the "occasional misdeeds" of some Christians pop up in the news?
3. How can the church earn the right to be heard?
4. In the video, Jeff posed the question, "How are you and your church community doing in following God's call to be salt and light in your community?" Discuss this question as honestly as you can.
5. What is your church doing well that you can build upon in order to serve more people more effectively?
6. What does your church need to do to become more like Jesus?
7. Discuss the paraphrased quote of Mother Teresa. How do small things done in love change the world?
8. Discuss Jeff's final questions: What small act can you take this week that will begin to make that change in the world? What big dream do you have for a lasting difference?

Review (3-5 minutes)

Help to solidify the content with participants by inviting them to name the three main points covered in this session. Ask volunteers to name them in their own words, assisting them as necessary.

In this session, the main points were:

1. Jesus calls his followers to be salt and light.
2. Choosing to serve God is one of the most meaningful choices you can ever make.
3. We can change the world with one act of love at a time.

Ask the following questions:

1. Why do we serve God? (Because Jesus calls us to, and because he modeled a life of service for us.)
2. How do we serve God? (Through small acts of love.)

Closing (5 minutes)

Remind participants that in the last video segment they heard a story about a New York cabbie who offered an inspired and eloquent homily of what the church would do if it were like Jesus. Ask participants to dream big about the ministries of your church:

1. How is the Holy Spirit stirring in you through this topic today?
2. How might you dream big about what God can do in and through you to serve others?
3. Make a commitment to pray, discern, and talk with others about joining or starting a ministry of service.

Pray Together (5 minutes)

Express gratitude for the commitment of the group members who have taken this journey to learn about serving God. Encourage them to continue praying for one another and dreaming together about serving God in ministry together.

Ask participants to share joys and concerns for the week. After a few minutes, close your time with a prayer of your own, or invite group members to pray in unison the prayer that is printed in the participant guide:

Heavenly Father, thank you for your great love for us. Thank you for inviting us into your work in the world. We know, Lord, that we are small. But by your power we can do great things. Create in us a vision for ministry. Show us how you would have us serve. Give us the courage to step out of our comfort zones. Forgive us when we withdraw and retreat from your call. Help us to be brave as we follow Jesus. In Jesus' name. Amen.

WALKING IT OUT

Encourage participants to take what they have learned today and apply it in their daily lives by reflecting on the "Walking It Out" page in the participant guide throughout the coming week.

NOTES

Session 3: Generosity

    1. The RESET Worksheet was created by Rev. Dr. Clayton Smith of The United Methodist Church of the Resurrection.

Session 4: Spiritual Gifts

    1. Madeleine L'Engle, *Choices for Graduates* (Grand Rapids: Baker, 1988), 26.